Sound It Out

Consonants

by Wiley Blevins
illustrated by Sean O'Neill

BOOKS™

Red Chair Press   Egremont, Massachusetts

Look! Books are produced and published by Red Chair Press:

Red Chair Press LLC   PO Box 333   South Egremont, MA 01258-0333

www.redchairpress.com

 FREE activity page from www.redchairpress.com/free-activities

Wiley Blevins is an early-reading specialist and author of the best-selling *Phonics from A to Z: A Practical Guide* from Scholastic and *A Fresh Look at Phonics* from Corwin. Wiley has taught elementary school in both the United States and in South America. He has written more than 70 books for children and 15 for teachers, as well as created reading programs for schools in the U.S. and Asia.

Publisher's Cataloging-In-Publication Data

Names: Blevins, Wiley. | O'Neill, Sean, 1968- illustrator.

Title: Consonants / by Wiley Blevins ; illustrated by Sean O'Neill.

Description: Egremont, Massachusetts : Red Chair Press, [2019] | Series: Look! books : Sound it out | Includes word-building examples. | Interest age level: 004-008. | Summary: "The alphabet has 26 letters -- 21 of them are consonants. They can be combined with vowels to build words. Readers discover what some of the most common consonants can do."--Provided by publisher.

Identifiers: ISBN 9781634403368 (library hardcover) | ISBN 9781634403481 (paperback) | ISBN 9781634403429 (ebook)

Subjects: LCSH: English language--Consonants--Juvenile literature. | English language--Pronunciation--Juvenile literature. | CYAC: English language--Consonants. | English language--Pronunciation.

Classification: LCC PE1159 .B54 2019 (print) | LCC PE1159 (ebook) | DDC 428.13--dc23

LCCN: 2017963409

Illustrations by Sean O'Neill

Photo credits: iStock

Printed in the United States of America

0918   1P CGBS19

Our alphabet has 26 letters.

5 of these letters are vowels.

A-E-I-O-U

The rest are called consonants.

Let's see what these consonants can do.

Table of Contents

Mm

Some consonants have sounds that can be stretched like a rubber band. Put your lips together. Say the sound for <u>m</u>. It's the first sound you hear in <u>milk</u>.

Mmmm

M

Man. Mouse. Monster.

Ss

See the snake. It slithers in the grass.

Say the sound for s. It's the first sound you hear in snake.
Ssss
S

Sun.
Sad.
Sandwich.

Ff

Feel the fan.
Fresh air for all!

Put your top teeth
on your bottom lip.
Say the sound for f.
It's the first sound
you hear in fan.
Ffff
F

Fun. Fox. Friend.

L l

Lick that lollipop.
Lots and lots of licks!
Say the sound for <u>l</u>.
It's the first sound
you hear in <u>lick</u>.
Llll
L

Leaf. Lunch. Love.

Nn

No! No! No!

I am <u>not</u> going to do it!

Say the sound for <u>n</u>. It's the first sound you hear in <u>no</u>. Now hold your nose and say the sound. Can you do it?

No!

Nnnn

N

Nest. Nice. Nine.

What a
nice nest.

Rr

The red race car
revs its engine.
Ready. Set. Go!

Say the sound for r.
It's the first sound
you hear in red.
Rrrr
R

Run. Race. Robot.

Pp

Some consonants have sounds
that can't be stretched. Hold your
hand in front of your mouth.
Now say the sound for p̲. It's
the first sound you hear in p̲o̲p̲!
What do you feel? A puff of air!
Say the sound many times fast:
"p" "p" "p".
P

Pig. Pencil. Popping popcorn.

Tt

Tick. Tock.
The clock tells time.
Say the sound for <u>t</u>.
It's the first sound
you hear in <u>time</u>.
Say the sound
many times fast:
"t" "t" "t".
T

Top. Tiger. Tornado.

Cc

Click. Click. Click.
Get your camera ready
for a pic!

Say the sound for <u>c</u>. It's
the first sound you hear in
<u>camera</u>. Say the sound many
times fast:
"c" "c" "c".
C

Cat. Cute. Clown.

Bb

Bounce that big ball.

Bounce it fast.

Bounce it against a wall.

Say the sound for <u>b</u>. It's the first sound you hear in <u>ball</u>. Say the sound many times fast: "b" "b" "b".

B

Big. Bear. Boy.

Dd

Dinosaurs dance around the desk. Tap, tap, wiggle, and dip.

Say the sound for <u>d</u>. It's the first sound you hear in <u>dinosaur</u>. Say the sound many times fast: "d" "d" "d".
D

Dog. Dad. Dandelion.

Let's Build Words

These are some of the consonants. Let's make words with them. The consonants plus a vowel are all we need. Ready, set, read!

Say the sound for <u>m</u>.
Now say the sound for <u>a</u>.
Put the two together: <u>ma</u>.
Add the sound for <u>d</u>
to the end.

What word did you make?
mad

Uh-oh! Dad is mad.
What did you do?

A mad Dad.

Say the sound for s̲.
Now say the sound for i̲.
Put the two together: s̲i̲.
Add the sound for t̲
to the end.

What word did you make?
sit

Go on. Sit and read a book.
Why not this one?
Give it another look!

Our alphabet has 26 letters.
5 of these letters are vowels.

A-E-I-O-U

The rest are called **consonants**.
Now you know what these
consonants can do.